D1497753

Pebble® Plus

Endangered and Threatened Animals

by Abbie Dunne

CAPSTONE PRESS
a capstone imprint

Pebble Plus is published by Capstone Press,
1710 Roe Crest Drive, North Mankato, Minnesota 56003
www.mycapstone.com

Library of Congress Cataloging-in-Publication Data
Names: Dunne, Abbie, author.
Title: Endangered and threatened animals / by Abbie Dunne.
Description: North Mankato, Minnesota : Capstone Press, [2017] | Series:
    Pebble plus. Life science | Audience: Ages 4-8.? | Audience: K to grade
    3.? | Includes bibliographical references and index.
Identifiers: LCCN 2016005322| ISBN 9781515709459 (library binding) | ISBN
    9781515709770 (pbk.) | ISBN 9781515711124 (ebook pdf)
Subjects: LCSH: Endangered species--Juvenile literature. | Wildlife
    conservation--Juvenile literature.
Classification: LCC QH75 .D86 2017 | DDC 591.68--dc23
LC record available at http://lccn.loc.gov/2016005322

Editorial Credits
Linda Staniford, editor; Bobbie Nuytten, designer; Jo Miller, media researcher;
Tori Abraham, production specialist

Photo Credits
Capstone Studio: Karon Dubke, 21; Dreamstime: Vishwa Kiran, 17; Newscom: Design Pics/Dave Fleetham,
19; Minden Pictures/FLPA/Michael Gore, 11; Shutterstock: Alexandra Giese, 5, Amy Nichole Harris, 13, hans
engbers, 7, Karel Gallas, cover, Matt Gibson, 1, Prezoom.nl, 15, tristan tan, 9

Design Elements
Shutterstock: Alena P

Note to Parents and Teachers

The Life Science set supports national curriculum standards for science. This book introduces
the concept of endangered and threatened animals. The images support early readers
in understanding the text. The repetition of words and phrases helps early readers in
understanding the text. This book also introduces early readers to subject-specific vocabulary
words, which are defined in the Glossary section. Early readers may need assistance to read
some words and to use the Table of Contents, Glossary, Read More, Internet Sites, Critical
Thinking Using the Common Core, and Index sections of the book.

Printed and bound in China.
007691

Table of Contents

Threatened, Endangered, and Extinct

Many animals in our world are thriving. But some are threatened or endangered. Threatened animals could soon be endangered. Endangered animals are close to dying out.

If all of one kind of animal dies, that animal is extinct. Dinosaurs are extinct. There are no longer any dinosaurs living on Earth.

Habitats

A habitat is where an animal lives.
Habitat loss or damage is hard
on animals. Trees in rain forests are
being cut down. The orangutans
who live there are endangered.

People damage animal habitats.

Oil polluted sea otter habitat
in Alaska. Many otters died.

Now sea otters are endangered.

Hunting

Some people hunt animals for food or fur. Too much hunting can endanger animals. People hunt rhinoceroses for their horns. Now rhinos are endangered.

Some people catch wild animals to sell as pets. Many great green macaws have been caught. Now they are endangered in the wild.

Saving Endangered Animals

Parks and reserves protect animals. Without them, some animals would die out. Gir National Park in India protects endangered Asiatic lions.

Scientists study animals
in their habitats. They try
to find out why the animals
are endangered. They can
help some animals survive.

Activity

A model is a small copy of something. It helps us see things we may not be able to easily spot. Make a model to show how animals can become extinct. Use the chart below.

ANIMAL	ENDANGERED	THREATENED	NO CONCERN
anhinga			X
black vulture			X
blue jay			X
cardinal			X
piping plover		X	
scrub jay		X	
snail kite	X		
wild turkey			X
wood stork	X		
wood warbler	X		

What You Need

- pencil
- strips of paper
- box

What You Do

1. Write the name of each bird of no concern on six strips of paper.

2. Write the name of each bird that is threatened on two strips of paper.

3. Write the name of each bird that is endangered on one strip of paper.

4. Put all of the strips in a box. Mix them up. Draw 20 strips of paper out of the box. These birds are in a new habitat that does not meet their needs. They do not survive.

5. Look in the box to see if any birds became extinct or are very close to becoming extinct.

What Do You Think?

Make a claim.

A claim is something you believe to be true.

What kind of event can lead animals to become extinct?

Use your model to support your claim.

21

Glossary

endangered—in danger of dying out

extinct—no longer living; an extinct animal is one that has died out, with no more of its kind

habitat—the natural place and conditions where a plant or animal lives

pollute—to make something dirty or unsafe

rain forest—a thick forest where rain falls nearly every day

reserve—land that is protected so that animals may live there safely

survive—to stay alive

threatened—in danger of becoming endangered

thrive—to live easily and well

Read More

Burnham, Cathleen. *Doyli to the Rescue: Saving Baby Monkeys in the Amazon.* Milwaukee, WI: Crickhollow Books, 2015.

Cohn, Jessica. *Protecting Animals.* Hand to Paw. Huntington Beach, CA: Teacher Created Materials, 2013.

Rice, Bill. *Endangered Animals of the Jungle.* Huntington Beach, CA: Teacher Created Materials, 2013.

Internet Sites

FactHound offers a safe, fun way to find Internet sites related to this book. All of the sites on FactHound have been researched by our staff.

Here's all you do:

Visit *www.facthound.com*

Type in this code: 9781515709459

Check out projects, games and lots more at
www.capstonekids.com

Critical Thinking Using the Common Core

1. What is a habitat? (Key Ideas and Details)

2. Dinosaurs are extinct. Explain what extinct means. (Key Ideas and Details)

3. Hunting is one way animals can become endangered. Can you name two other ways? (Integration of Knowledge and Ideas)

4. Why do you think parks and reserves help save endangered animals? (Integration of Knowledge and Ideas)

Index